COUNTRY LIVING

Crafting
Vintage Style

COUNTRY LIVING

Crafting
Vintage Style

*Charming Projects
for Home and Garden*

CHRISTINA STRUTT

HEARST BOOKS
A DIVISION OF STERLING PUBLISHING CO., INC.
NEW YORK

Library of Congress Cataloging-in-Publication Data
Strutt, Christina
    Country living crafting vintage style: charming projects for home and garden / Christina Strutt.
        p. cm.
Includes index
    ISBN 1-58816-241-9
    1. Textile crafts. 2. Home furnishings. I. Title: Crafting vintage style. II. Country living (New York, N.Y.) III. Title.
    TT699.S784 2003
    746—dc21

10 9 8 7 6 5 4 3 2 1

First Paperback Edition 2005
Published by Hearst Books
A Division of Sterling Publishing Co., Inc.
387 Park Avenue South, New York, NY 10016

Country Living is a trademark owned by Hearst Magazines Property, Inc., in USA, and Hearst Communications, Inc., in Canada. Hearst Books is a trademark owned by Hearst Communications, Inc.

www.countryliving.com

Distributed in Canada by Sterling Publishing
c/o Canadian Manda Group, One Atlantic Avenue, Suite 105
Toronto, Ontario, Canada M6K 3E7

Distributed in Australia by Capricorn Link (Australia) Pty. Ltd.
P.O. Box 704, Windsor, NSW 2756 Australia

Printed in Thailand

ISBN 1-58816-428-4

Edited by Sarah Hoggett
Illustrations by Kate Simunek
Photography by Edina van der Wyck
Designed by Christine Wood

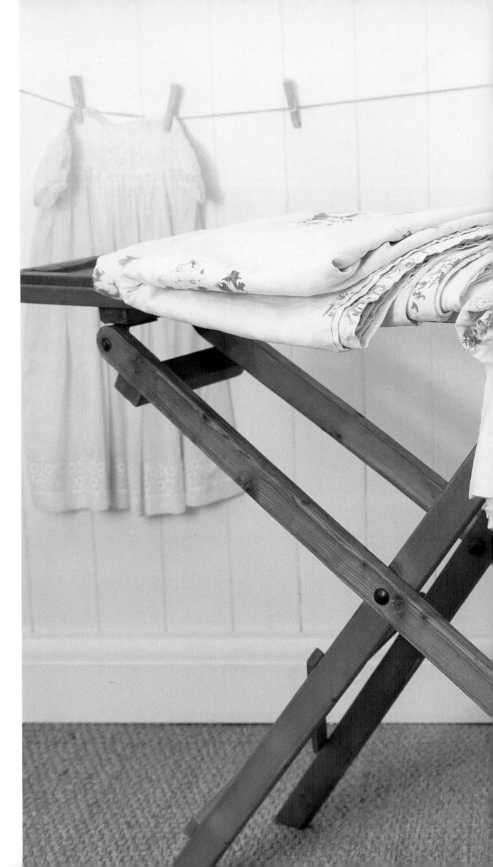

contents

foreword

I am a big fan of simple projects, particularly those that don't require special skills, unusual tools, or expensive materials. In this book we feature 30 such projects—each one beautifully illustrated with easy-to-follow instructions and most requiring no special crafting or sewing talents. Best of all, you can transform inexpensive thrift store finds or remnant fabrics into beautiful, practical accessories for your home or create as a gift for someone special.

In *Crafting Vintage Style*, you'll discover how simple—and satisfying—it is to bring hand-made beauty into your home. Consider reviving an old, discarded deck chair with a beautiful floral fabric (see page 86). Or create an unusual display for cards and notes by using old-fashioned, wooden clothespins (page 40). There's an easy-to-make laundry bag, a decorative window treatment, and a heart-shape cushion too. If you're looking for something special for the holidays, there's a warm red flannel skirt that is certain to make the season festive and bright (page 62).

I hope you find the projects in this book as inspiring as I did. Enjoy!

NANCY MERNIT SORIANO
EDITOR-IN-CHIEF, *COUNTRY LIVING*

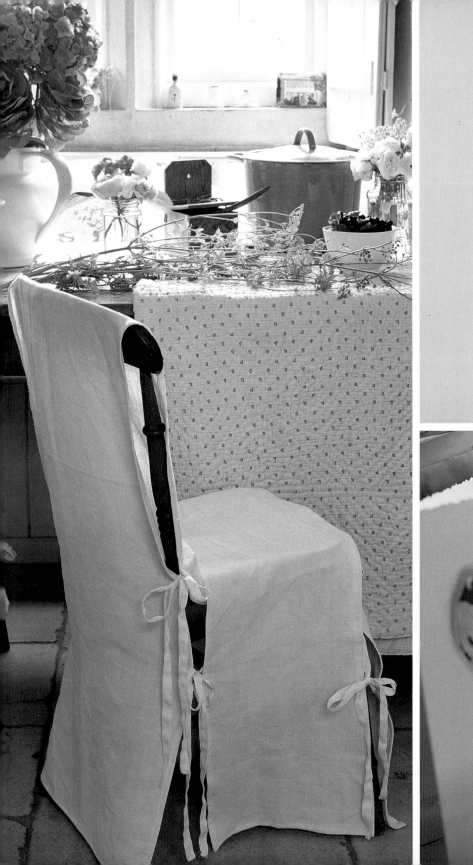

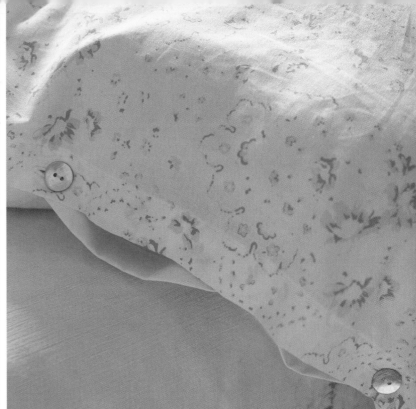

CRAFTING FOR THE VINTAGE HOME

From tiny lavender sachets made from scraps of vintage fabrics to cozy cushions and delicate, full-length muslin curtains, this chapter contains a host of simple yet stylish ideas for every room of the house. Both functional and decorative, these delightful projects will add a touch of vintage romance to any home.

scalloped shelf edging

A simple fabric edging can transform a shelf from utilitarian storage to attractive display unit in an instant. Here we have used a vintage French check, which always looks perfectly at home wherever you use it. Alternatively, you could use pretty paper. Wallpaper is particularly suitable, as you can cut long lengths from a single roll, provided the pattern looks as good horizontally as it does vertically.

MATERIALS

paper for template

pencil

*fabric the same width as your shelf and approx.
4-in. (10-cm) deep*

cotton bias tape ½-in. (1-cm) wide for binding

needle and thread or sewing machine

small length of ¾-in. (2-cm) Velcro

pins

1 Measure the shelf and cut a piece of paper large enough to make a template for the edging. In this case, the shelf edging follows a half-moon shape which can be made by drawing around half a cake tin; to make the shapes fall evenly, fold the paper as many times as your space allows, draw the pattern on one segment only, and cut through the folded paper so that the shapes fall evenly along the shelf.

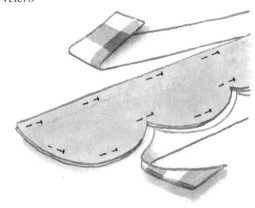

2 Unfold the paper and pin it on the fabric. Cut out the fabric following the paper pattern.

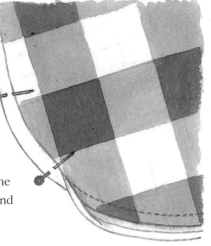

3 With the right side of the edging facing upward, pin bias tape along the raw edges. Stitch all around about ¼ in. (6 mm) from the edge, removing the pins as you go. Fold the tape over to the wrong side, pin in place, and stitch along the edge.

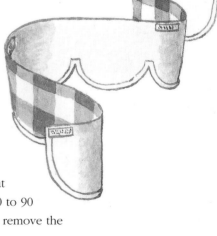

4 Sew the smooth side of a 1-in. (2.5-cm) length of Velcro to the fabric and stick the gripper side to the top edge of the shelf, taking care to align the two halves accurately. Repeat this at intervals of 2 to 3 ft. (60 to 90 cm). This allows you to remove the shelf edging for washing.

simple slipcovers

These stylish slipcovers are a quick-and-easy way
to revamp dining chairs that have seen better days.
Use cotton or canvas fabrics, which are strong but easily
washable, or antique linen sheets as we have done here. Still
available in markets and thrift stores, the linen is hand made
from sturdy flax and will withstand heavy wear and tear.

MATERIALS

cotton, canvas, or linen
fabric for covers

¼ yd. (0.25 m) matching
fabric or
2 yds (180 cm) of
1-in. (2.5-cm) grosgrain
ribbon for ties

sewing machine

needle and matching
thread

tape measure

tailor's chalk

pins

1 Measure your chair from front to back, starting at the foot of the back legs and going up and over the back and seat to the foot of the front legs. Take a second measurement from side to side, going from the foot of the front leg up and over the seat and down to the foot of the opposite leg. Cut out one piece of fabric to each measurement, adding 1 in. (2.5 cm) all around on each piece for hems.

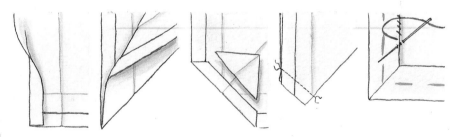

2 To miter the corners, fold the hems over twice, and press. Open the fabric flat, turn back the corner triangle at 45°, and press. Open the corner again, fold it diagonally, right sides together, so that the raw edges and the creases meet, and press. Trim the seam allowance from the corner and press the seam open. Fold the hems over and pin or baste in place. Hem by hand using tiny slipstitches or by machine.

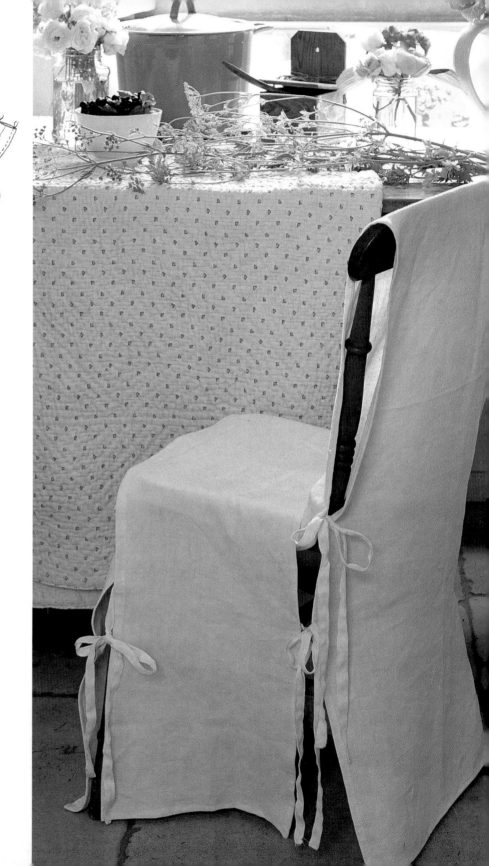

3 To make the fabric ties, cut the fabric into sixteen 12 x 2½ in. (30 x 6 cm) lengths, fold each strip in half right sides together, and stitch the sides and one short edge. Turn right side out and slipstitch the other short edge to close. To make ribbon ties, simply cut the grosgrain into 12-in. (30-cm) lengths.

4 Lay the two hemmed fabric pieces in position on the chair, and pin them together at the points where the ties will be fixed. Mark the position of each set of ties with tailor's chalk. Pin each set of ties in place, making sure each tie matches up accurately with its opposing number, and stitch firmly in place.

summer curtain

These light and airy curtains are the perfect choice for the summer months, when the sun can stream into your bedroom early in the morning and welcome in the new day! Our curtain was made from fine cotton muslin printed with a faded rose pattern, which suits this type of curtain perfectly. The ties were made from cotton bias tape, although you might prefer to make them from the same fabric as the curtain.

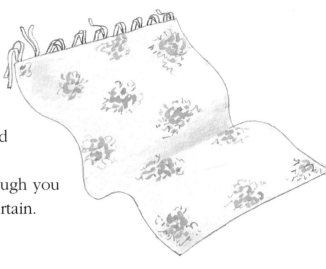

MATERIALS

fine cotton muslin fabric
cotton bias tape ½-in. (1-cm) wide
tape measure
sewing machine
needle and matching thread

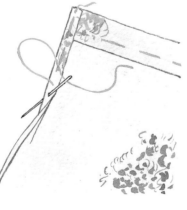

1 To work out how much fabric you will need, measure from the top of your curtain pole to the floor, adding 2 in. (5 cm) to the length for hems, and from one side of the window to the other, multiplying this measurement by 1.5 to 2 times. Cut out the fabric to this measurement. Hem the top and sides.

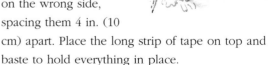

2 Cut one piece of tape the width of the curtain and 9- to 10-in. (22- to 25-cm) lengths of tape for the ties. Place the curtain right side down and pin the lengths of tape in pairs on the wrong side, spacing them 4 in. (10 cm) apart. Place the long strip of tape on top and baste to hold everything in place.

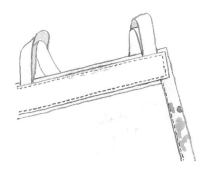

3 Machine stitch around all edges of the tape, catching in both ends of each tie as you go. Hem the bottom of the curtain.

4 Tie the curtain on the pole with neat bows, with the first bow between the pole support and the finial.

basin skirt

Dress up a washbasin and give yourself extra concealed storage space for cleaning materials or other bathroom essentials with this pretty, easy-to-make skirt. To complete the look, you could make coordinating curtains, or edge white or cream towels with the same fabric.

MATERIALS

Cotton fabric

Elastic ¾ in. (2 cm) wide

Tape measure

Approx. 8–10 in. (20–25 cm) Velcro cut into 1 in. (2.5-cm) pieces

Needle and thread

2 safety pins

PVA glue

1 Measure the basin from the back of wall right around the front of the basin to the other side and double this measurement. Measure the height of the basin, adding an extra 2 in. (5 cm) top and bottom. Cut out a piece of fabric to this measurement.

2 Along the sides of the fabric, fold over ½ in. (1 cm) and then another ½ in. (1 cm) to make a double hem, and stitch. Hem the bottom of the fabric in this way.

3 Along the top edge of the fabric, fold over ½ in. (1 cm) and then another 1 in. (2.5 cm) to make a slot for the elastic and stitch. Attach a safety pin to each end of the elastic, thread it through the slot, and gather evenly. Secure the elastic at both ends with sturdy stitches.

4 Sew each Velcro piece to the top of the skirt. Aligning the pieces carefully, stick the opposite side of the Velcro to the basin using PVA glue.

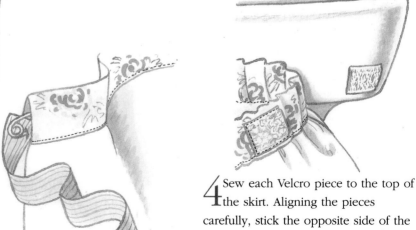

heart-shape cushion

This delightful little heart-shape cushion could grace any room in the home. Shown here on a comfortable kitchen chair painted to match one of the colors in the cushion fabric, it would look equally at home on a calico-covered sofa or a crisp cotton waffle bedspread.

MATERIALS

brown paper for templates

pencil

tailor's chalk

13 x 28 in. (33 x 71 cm) of lining fabric

feathers, synthetic stuffing, or other stuffing of your choice

14 x 30 in. (36 x 76 cm) of fabric for cushion cover

sewing machine

needle and matching thread

snaps

pins

1 To make a pattern for the cushion pad, fold a piece of brown paper in half and draw one half of a heart shape along the folded edge. Open out the pattern, place it on one half of the lining fabric, and draw around it with a soft pencil (this is the stitching line). Cut out two pieces of lining fabric, cutting ½ in. (1 cm) outside the drawn line.

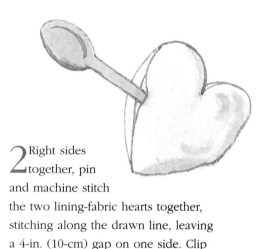

2 Right sides together, pin and machine stitch the two lining-fabric hearts together, stitching along the drawn line, leaving a 4-in. (10-cm) gap on one side. Clip the corners and curves, taking care not to cut through the stitching. Turn the pad right side out, stuff to the desired fullness, and slipstitch the gap closed.

3 Make a paper pattern for the cover that is 1 in. (2.5 cm) larger all around than the pattern for the cushion pad. Fold in half, then fold a generous overlap. Cut one piece for the front, using the full pattern. Fold the pattern to the overlap and cut two back pieces. Mark the center foldline on each back piece.

4 Turn under and machine stitch a narrow double hem on the raw straight edge of each back piece. Place the back pieces on the front piece, right sides together, and machine stitch all around the outside edge taking a ½-in (1-cm) seam. Turn the cushion cover right side out, stitch snaps along the central overlap, and insert the cushion pad.

beaded pot cover

A row of these pretty covers will add instant color and interest to any kitchen, or you could use the covers as attractive little table covers. As you only need small pieces of fabric, this project is an ideal way to use up fabric scraps; you could create a set of covers in contrasting prints.

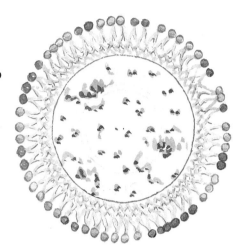

MATERIALS

pretty vintage-style fabrics
lengths of lace or crochet trim
beads or heavy buttons
tailor's chalk
needle and thread
pins

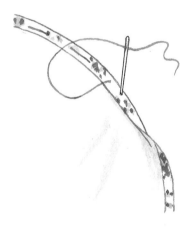

1 Find a saucer or plate that is about 3 to 4 in. (7.5 to 10 cm) larger in circumference than the jar or pot that you want to cover, place it on the wrong side of your fabric, and draw around it with tailor's chalk or a soft pencil. Cut out the fabric circle. Cut a length of lace or crochet trim long enough to go around the circumference of the fabric circle.

2 Turn under a ¼-in. (6-mm) double hem on the wrong side of the fabric circle and baste (you may need to make small gathers as you go).

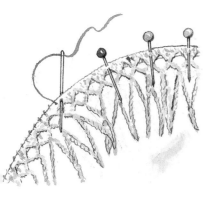

3 Pin the lace or crochet trim to the wrong side of the fabric circle and stitch it to the fabric using tiny slipstitches.

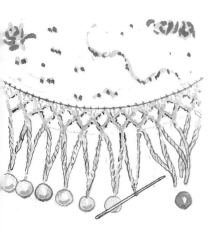

4 Sew beads or buttons onto the edge of the lace or crochet trim at regular intervals.

storage boxes

These pretty fabric-covered boxes are the perfect way to house papers, stationery, and other essential items and to conceal clutter. Arranged on shelves, they make a stylish and elegant display in their own right and are a simple alternative to cupboards and filing cabinets.

Fabric is easier to use than paper, as it is pliable and fits into corners more neatly than stiff paper. It needs to be thick enough to disguise the original box, but not so thick as to make a lumpy finish.

MATERIALS

sturdy box with lid
patterned fabric
spray adhesive or fabric glue
16 in. (40 cm) of ¼-in. (6-mm) ribbon
decorative patterned paper (optional)

1 Lay your box on the fabric to work out how much you need. Cut two pieces of fabric — one to cover the outside of the box and one to cover the inside, allowing ½-in. (1-cm) overlap all around on both pieces.

2 Fold the hems over and press to make a crease. Unfold. Fold the corner over at 45° and crease. Unfold. Cut diagonally across the corner where the creases meet. Working in a well-ventilated area, apply glue to the outside of the box. Press the fabric on firmly, smoothing out any wrinkles. Repeat for the inside of the box.

3 Take an 8-in. (20-cm) length of ribbon and fold it in half. At the point where the ribbon is folded, glue it firmly to the center of the inside of the lid, and the other to the center of the outside of the lid.

4 Take a second length of ribbon and glue it to the middle of the front of the box in the same way. If the inside of the box is not as neat as you would like, cut out pieces of decorative paper to the correct size and glue them in place.

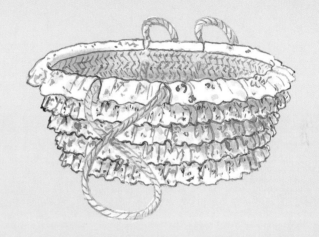

fabric-covered basket

Strips of soft cotton transform this ordinary, store-bought shopping basket into a delicately textured, feminine-looking and useful shopper.

   You need a basket with a fairly loose weave for this project, otherwise it will be difficult to get the needle through without damaging the basket. You can use either the same fabric throughout, or mix and match fabrics for variety.

MATERIALS

woven straw shopping basket
long strips of cotton
needle and thread

1 Tear long strips of fabric about 2-in. (5-cm) wide.

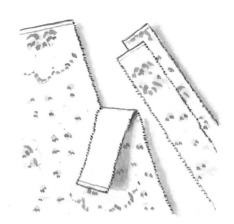

2 Run one row of running stitches along the top of each strip, pulling the thread to gather the fabric slightly as you go.

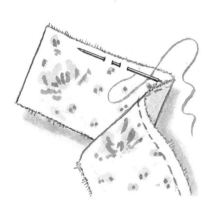

3 Starting at the bottom of the basket, fold over the top of each fabric strip and stitch it to the outside of the basket, taking the needle through holes in the basket weave.

4 When you reach the top of the basket, sew the last strip to the inside to the basket and then flip it over to the outside so that you get a neat top edge.

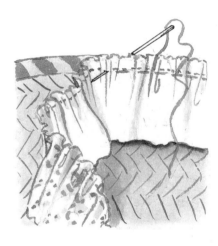

greeting cards

There is something very touching about receiving a homemade card and knowing that someone has taken the time and trouble to make it especially for you. These designs use simple shapes that anyone can draw and have a naïve charm that is very appealing.

MATERIALS

good-quality card or thick, handmade paper

scraps of vintage fabric

needle and matching thread

spray adhesive or fabric glue

1 Cut the card or paper to the required size and carefully fold along the center.

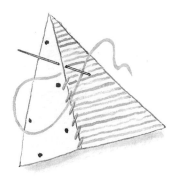

2 For a boat picture, cut two sail shapes of triangles, fold fabric over to the wrong side to get a neat edge, and sew them together by whipstitching along the edge. Cut a contrasting piece of fabric for the base and sew to the sails in the same way.

3 Working in a well-ventilated area, stick the fabric boat to the card. We have sewn running stitches onto the card to mimic a wave in the sea, although you could draw or paint this line if you prefer.

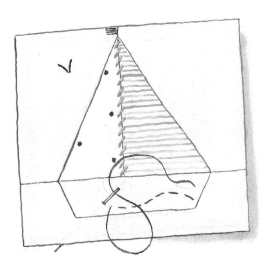

4 For a romantic alternative, cut two heart shapes from printed muslin. Stitch them together, leaving a small opening, and loosely fill the bag with lavender or rose petals. Stitch the opening closed, and attach the heart to your card.

cozy cushions

Give old cushions a new lease on life by covering the pads with vintage fabric. The striped ticking cushion shown on the right uses lovely antique mother-of-pearl buttons found in a thrift store but, if sewing is not your strong point, you could simply stitch together two squares of fabric and attach ribbon or fabric ties.

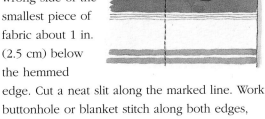

MATERIALS

One piece of fabric the same size as your cushion pad plus 2 in. (5 cm) all around

One piece of fabric half the size of your cushion pad plus 1½ in. (4 cm) all around

One piece of fabric two-thirds the size of your cushion pad plus 1½ in. (4 cm) all around

3 or 4 buttons or 4 x 9-in (23-cm) lengths of 1-in. (2.5-cm) ribbon to tie

tailor's chalk

sewing machine

needle and matching thread

pins

1 Cut out fabric following the measurements given in the materials list. Hem one long side of each of the two smallest pieces of fabric.

2 Mark the position of the buttonholes with tailor's chalk on the wrong side of the smallest piece of fabric about 1 in. (2.5 cm) below the hemmed edge. Cut a neat slit along the marked line. Work buttonhole or blanket stitch along both edges, finishing with a few straight stitches to secure.

3 Lay the second largest piece of fabric on a table, right side up, and place the smallest piece on top of it, with the hemmed edges in the center and the buttonhole edge overlapping the larger piece of fabric by about 2 in. (5 cm).

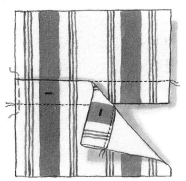

4 Place the largest piece of fabric on top of the other two, right sides together. Taking a ½-in. (1-cm) seam, machine stitch around the outer edges, leaving the overlapping section unsewn. Turn the cushion cover right side out. Insert a pin through the center of each buttonhole into the second largest piece of fabric and sew on a button at each of these points.

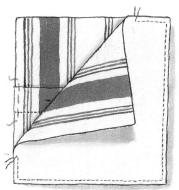

clothespin boards

These boards are a wonderfully simple way of storing things that are pretty enough to be on display for a while, such as postcards, magazine cuttings, and invitations that might slip out of mind if they are out of sight. If you're not confident about your woodworking skills, ask your lumber merchant to cut the wood and drill the screw holes for you.

MATERIALS

wooden board measuring 16 x 4 ½ x ¾ in. (41 x 11 x 2 cm)

drill and ¼-in. (6-mm) bit

matte latex (emulsion) paint

pencil

strong wood glue

3 wooden pegs

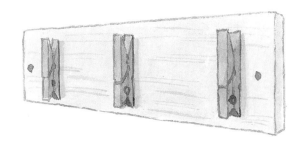

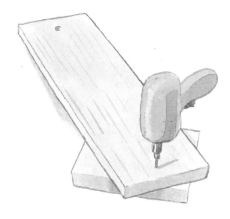

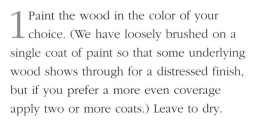

1 Paint the wood in the color of your choice. (We have loosely brushed on a single coat of paint so that some underlying wood shows through for a distressed finish, but if you prefer a more even coverage apply two or more coats.) Leave to dry.

2 Place a spare piece of wood beneath the peg board to protect your working surface and drill one screw hole in the center of each short side of the peg board, 1 in. (2.5 cm) in from the edge.

3 Lightly mark the position of the pins on the board in pencil, spacing them equally. Apply strong wood glue to one side of each clothespin and fix each one firmly in position.

dog blanket

Store-bought dog blankets and basket linings can be very expensive, so this project is a great way of saving money by using up an old blanket and fabric remnants. For an even softer, more luxurious version, you could cover an old crib quilt or large, battered cushion following the instructions for the duvet cover on pages 46–49.

MATERIALS

34 x 29 in. (86 x 74 cm) strong cotton fabric

34 x 29 in. (86 x 74 cm) lightweight blanket for the backing

sewing machine

needle and matching thread

1 Place the cotton fabric on top of the blanket, right sides together, and pin around the edges.

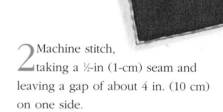

2 Machine stitch, taking a ½-in (1-cm) seam and leaving a gap of about 4 in. (10 cm) on one side.

3 Turn the piece right side out and slipstich the gap closed.

4 If you wish, pin the two layers together and stitch along a simple grid pattern over the whole pieces, spacing the stitching lines about 3 in. (7.5 cm) apart, to prevent the two pieces from slipping.

dog bowl mat

No matter how much you love your pet, the clatter of a food bowl on tiles as dear little Fido tries to lap up every last morsel of his dinner is not the most musical sound in the world—not to mention the damage it can do to your flooring! This ingenious mat provides the perfect solution: not only does it prevent the bowl from slipping around, it can also be wiped clean in an instant.

MATERIALS

Piece of wood approx.
14 x 12 x ½ in.
(36 cm x 30 x 1.5 cm)

Oilcloth—one piece measuring
18 x 16 in. (46 cm x 41 cm),
one piece measuring 13 x 11 in.
(33 cm x 28 cm)

Scissors

Pencil

Spray adhesive

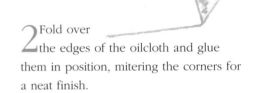

1 Place the larger piece of oilcloth wrong side up, center the wood on it, and draw around it in pencil to mark the position. Working in a well-ventilated area and wearing a face mask and protective gloves, spray adhesive on one side of the wood. Place it sticky side down on the larger piece of oilcloth, aligning it with the pencil marks.

2 Fold over the edges of the oilcloth and glue them in position, mitering the corners for a neat finish.

3 Apply spray adhesive the the uncovered wood and folded-over oilcloth, and place the smaller piece of oilcloth on top, smoothing out any wrinkles and pressing it down firmly to secure it in place.

herbal slumber pillow

Filled with dried lavender (or any other sweet-scented dried herb of your choice), these little pillows are a heavenly soporific, soothing away the stresses of the day and gently lulling you to sleep. Because of their size, they are a good way of using up old scraps of fabric and can be embellished with pretty buttons or ribbon to fasten.

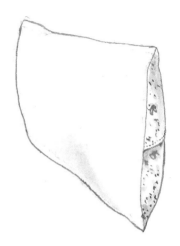

MATERIALS

19 x 9½-in. (48 x 24 cm) of lining fabric for cushion pad
filling of your choice
muslin sachet of dried lavender, rose petals, or other herb
10-in. (25-cm) square of cotton or linen for front of cushion
10 x 6 in. (25 x 15 cm) cotton or linen for first back piece
10 x 7 in. (25 x 17.5 cm) cotton or linen for second back piece
needle and matching thread
button or length of ribbon to fasten
pins

1 Fold the rectangle of lining fabric in half lengthwise, right sides together, and stitch around the open edges, leaving a 4-in. (10-cm) gap in one side. Turn right side out and fill, burying the herb sachet in the center, and slipstitch the gap closed.

2 Hem one long side of each of the back pieces. If you are fastening the cushion with a button, make a buttonhole in the center of the smaller of the two back pieces, following the instructions on page 38.

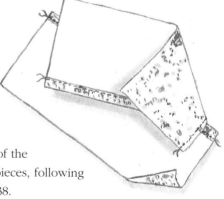

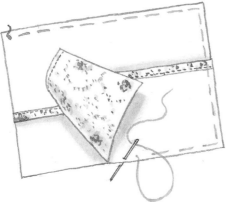

3 Lay the two back pieces on top of the front of the cushion, right sides together, with the hemmed sides overlapping in the middle and the smaller back piece overlapping the larger one. Taking a ½-in. (1-cm) seam, sew the cushion together around the four outer edges and turn right side out.

4 Sew a button in the center of the opening. Alternatively, attach a piece of ribbon on each side of the opening to fasten.

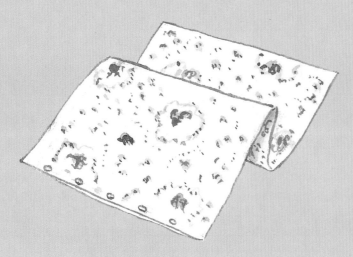

duvet cover

Whether you choose a fabric to match your curtains and other home furnishings or go for something with a strongly contrasting color or pattern, a new duvet cover can bring all the elements of a bedroom decorating scheme together.

The beauty of making your own duvet covers is that you have a far wider range of fabrics to choose from.

MATERIALS

cotton fabric
buttons (at least 6 for a duvet for a single bed)
sewing machine
needle and matching thread
pins

1 Cut two pieces of fabric to the length and width of the duvet, adding 6 in. (15 cm) to the length and 3 in. (7.5 cm) to the width for seam allowances and hems. If you need to join pieces of fabric to achieve the correct width, have one full width in the center and narrower pieces on either side to avoid having a seam running down the middle.

2 Right sides together, pin the two pieces together and stitch around both long and one short edges, taking a ½-in. (1-cm) seam. Cut diagonally across the corners to reduce the bulk.

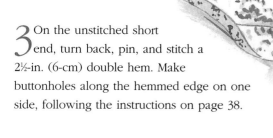

3 On the unstitched short end, turn back, pin, and stitch a 2½-in. (6-cm) double hem. Make buttonholes along the hemmed edge on one side, following the instructions on page 38.

4 Turn the duvet cover right side out. To mark the position of the buttons accurately, insert a pin through the center of each buttonhole. Stitch the buttons to the inside hemmed edge.

patchwork crib quilt

This patchwork quilt is a lovely way of using up worn denim jeans and other clothes that no longer fit or are out of fashion. Make sure the fabrics are all the same weight and that the grain runs in the same direction on each piece.

MATERIALS

squares and rectangles of coordinating pieces of soft denim or cotton for the quilt top

cotton fabric or lightweight blanket for the backing

sewing machine

needle and matching thread

pins (optional)

1 Lay out the pieces you have selected for the quilt top and move them around until you are happy with the arrangement. Turn under the raw edges by ¼ in. (6 mm) and press so that the fold lines are clearly visible.

2 Open up the fold and, right sides together, machine stitch along the fold lines (or hand stitch using tiny backstitches). Press each seam to one side as you finish it. When the quilt top is the size you want (ours measures 23 x 32 in./58 x 81 cm), trim the edges to make a neat rectangle.

3 Right sides together, stitch the patchwork top to a single piece of cotton fabric or blanket the same size as the quilt top, leaving a 6-in. (15-cm) gap in one side for turning. Turn the top right side out and slipstitch the gap closed.

4 If you wish, pin the two layers together and stitch along the seam lines to prevent the two pieces from slipping (this is known as quilting "in the ditch").

summer skirt

Made from a pretty floral print, these light cotton skirts are the
perfect way to keep cool on hot summer days.

MATERIALS

*Cotton fabric measuring
108 x 42 in.
(270 x 105 cm)*

*26 in. (66 cm) 1-in.
(2.5-cm) elastic*

Scissors

Needle and thread

2 safety pins

1 Fold the fabric in half, right sides
together, and stitch the sides. Press
open the seam.

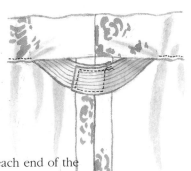

3 Attach a safety pin to each end of the
elastic and feed it through the slot.
Gather the fabric to the desired size and
stitch both ends of the elastic in position.

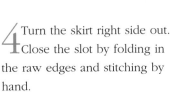

2 Hem the bottom edge
of the skirt by turning over ½
in. (1 cm) and then 1 in. (2.5 cm)
and stitch by hand or by machine.
Hem the top edge of the skirt by
turning over ½ in. (1 cm) and
then 1½ in. (3.5 cm) and stitch by
hand or by machine. Leave the
edge over the seam unstitched to
create an opening for the elastic.

4 Turn the skirt right side out.
Close the slot by folding in
the raw edges and stitching by
hand.

scented sachets

These pretty little sachets are filled with sweet-smelling lavender or rose petals. They make wonderful gifts to tuck into laundry closets or hang on coat hangers. If you don't have enough petals to fill the sachet, fill it with a stuffing of your choice, and then scent the stuffing with aromatherapy or pot-pourri oil.

MATERIALS

scraps of pretty vintage fabrics
dried lavender or rose petals (or filler and aromatherapy oil)
sewing machine or needle
matching thread
6-in. (15-cm) length of thin ribbon

1 Stitch scraps of fabric together to form two rectangles approximately 5½ x 3½ in. (14 x 9 cm).

2 Hem one short edge of each piece and place the two pieces right sides together. Taking a ¼-in. (6-mm) seam, machine stitch (or hand stitch, using tiny backstitches) around the three raw edges to join the two pieces of fabric together. Turn the bag right side out.

3 Fill the bag with your chosen filling, shaking it deep into the corners.

4 Gather the top of the bag and tie it with a ribbon in a contrasting color.

laundry bags

These delightful laundry bags will brighten up any utility room or
bathroom. Make several of them in different fabrics for each
member of the family. You can also use them as shoe bags
or as a way of storing small items such as scarves.

MATERIALS

2 pieces linen or heavy cotton, approx. 24 x 16 in. (60 x 40 cm)

1 strip linen or heavy cotton, approx. 16 x 2 in. (40 x 5 cm)

sewing machine

matching thread

1 yd. (1 m) cord

pins and large safety pin

1 Place the two pieces of fabric right sides together and stitch around three sides, taking a ¼-in. (6-mm) seam. Leave 1 in. (2.5 cm) unsewn at the open end for the hem.

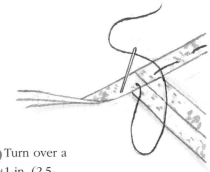

2 Turn over a 1-in. (2.5-cm) double hem on the open end and stitch by hand or machine, then sew up the sides of the bag. Turn the bag right sides out.

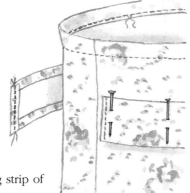

3 Fold over ½ in. (1 cm) of each long edge of the long strip of fabric to the wrong side and press. Starting about 2 in. (5 cm) down from the top edge and ½ in. (1 cm) from one seam, pin the strip around the bag and topstitch each edge. Leave the ends open.

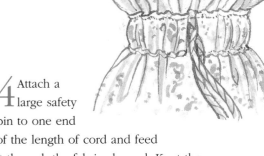

4 Attach a large safety pin to one end of the length of cord and feed it through the fabric channel. Knot the ends securely.

plaid teddy bear

This decorative teddy bear can be made from any type of fabric—cottons, linens, anything at all. Perhaps you have treasured clothes worn by your children that are not in a good enough condition to pass on to future generations? Making a teddy bear out of them is a lovely way to bring back happy memories.

MATERIALS

paper for making a template
pencil
two 12-in. (30-cm) square pieces of fabric
pins
tiny buttons or contrasting embroidery thread
filler of your choice
sewing machine
needle and matching thread
3-in. (7.5-cm) length of string

1 Draw a teddy-bear shape on paper and cut it out to make a template. Place your two fabric squares one on top of the other, pin the template on top, and cut out your teddy-bear shapes.

2 Sew tiny buttons on the front piece of the teddy bear or, if you're giving the teddy to a very young child, embroider little French knots in a contrasting color of thread.

3 Wrong sides together, machine stitch (or hand stitch using tiny backstitches) around the outline about ¼ in. (6 mm) in from the edge, leaving a gap of about 1 in. (2.5 cm) at the head. Fill the teddy bear with filler, using the blunt end of a pencil to push the filler down into the legs, and sew up the gap.

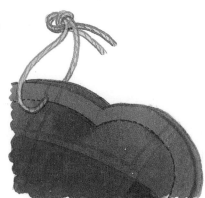

4 To hang up the teddy bear, attach a loop of string to the top of the head.

celebration skirt

The simple pattern of this skirt is flattering and suitable for all shapes and sizes, including children. Stylish but comfortable to wear, you can make it in soft, heavy winter flannel, or crisp cotton for summer.

MATERIALS

red flannel (see Step 1 for instructions on how to measure)

sewing machine

matching thread

strong 1-in. (2.5-cm) elastic

large safety pin

yarn or 2 strands of embroidery floss or wool in a contrasting color

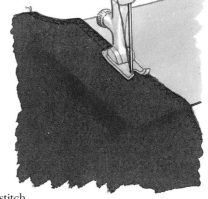

1 Decide what size you want to make the skirt and cut out two pieces, each one measuring the finished length plus 3 in. (7.5 cm) and about 2½ times the finished width. Overlock or zigzag stitch raw edges to prevent fraying. Taking a ½-in. (1-cm) seam, stitch the side edges together.

2 Turn over 2 in. (5 cm) on the top edge of the skirt and stitch to form a channel for the waistband, leaving a 1-in. (2.5-cm) gap on each side of one seam. Pin a large safety pin to one end of your length of elastic and feed the elastic through the channel until it comes out at the other end. Stitch the ends of the elastic together and slipstitch the gap in the waistband closed.

3 Turn over a 1-in. (2.5-cm) hem along the bottom edge of the skirt and stitch. Turn the skirt right side out. Embroider the hem of the skirt with the festive message or motif of your choice. Running stitch is a good choice for lettering: it is easy to do and has a simple, homespun charm.

tab-headed kitchen curtains

Blue and white is a lovely, fresh-looking color combination, and these gingham curtains bring a light, airy feel to a country-style kitchen. This is a variation on the Summer Curtains shown on pages 18–21, but because the fabric is slightly heavier a separate fabric facing is used to hold the tabs firmly in place. Tab-headed curtains do not need to be very full: a panel of fabric the width of the window plus a little extra for drape is sufficient.

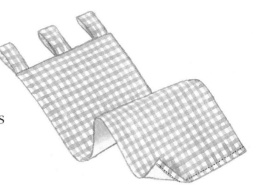

MATERIALS

For the curtain: panel of fabric measuring the width of the window plus 6 in. (15 cm) by the required length plus 4 in. (10 cm)

For the facing strip: strip of fabric the width of the window by 3 in. (7.5 cm)

For the tabs: strips of fabric measuring 12 x 6 in. (30 x 15 cm)

Tape measure

Scissors

Pins

Needle and matching thread

1 Fold over a 1-in. (2.5-cm) double hem along both sides of the curtain fabric and stitch. Hem the top and bottom edges in this way.

3 Zigzag-stitch one long edge of the facing strip. Place the facing strip on top of the curtain right sides together. Fold each tab in half widthwise with the seam sides together. Pin one tab flush with the right and left edges. Pin the rest of the tabs at 6-in. (15-cm) intervals between the curtain and the facing strip, right sides together and edges aligned.

2 Next, make the tabs. Fold each strip of fabric in half lengthwise, right sides together, and stitch along the raw long side. Turn right side out and press, centering the seam on the back.

4 Stitch along the top edge of the curtain, catching in both ends of each tab as you go, and along the short ends of the facing strip. Turn right sides out so that the facing is on the wrong side of the curtain and press.

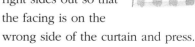

fabric roses

These charming fabric roses can be used to decorate any number of items—hats, bags and baskets, or even a large pin to make a flamboyant floral brooch. Tearing the fabric rather than cutting it gives a lovely, soft edge, just like the petals of real roses.

MATERIALS

muslin or cotton fabric

needle and matching thread

1 Tear muslin or cotton into strips that are about 5 ft. (150 cm) long and 2-in. (5-cm) wide.

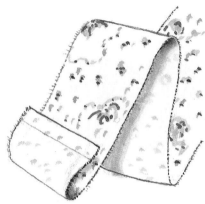

2 Thread a needle with a double length of thread and knot the end. Turn over about ½ in. (1 cm) to the wrong side to make a hem and sew a line of running stitches along the length of the fabric.

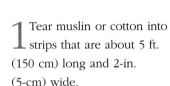
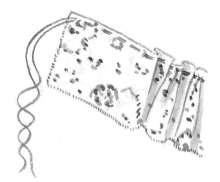

3 Pull up the thread, gathering the fabric evenly.

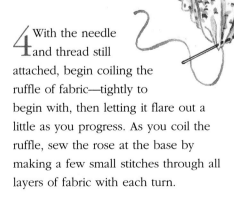

4 With the needle and thread still attached, begin coiling the ruffle of fabric—tightly to begin with, then letting it flare out a little as you progress. As you coil the ruffle, sew the rose at the base by making a few small stitches through all layers of fabric with each turn.

CRAFTING FOR THE VINTAGE GARDEN

Country picnics and afternoons lounging in a deck chair: the long, lazy days of summer are a time to unwind, and this section is packed with ideas to help you make the most of outdoor living. For the more energetic, a flower-printed gardener's apron adds a work-manlike touch to mundane chores, while a linen-covered journal is perfect for recording your triumphs through the gardening year.

gardener's apron

This voluminous apron has a generous cut and
storage capacity. Made from sturdy canvas, it has a
sectioned front pocket that is just the thing for all those lengths
of twine, gloves, and shears that you need as you go about
your garden chores.

MATERIALS

36 x 29 in. (92 x 74 cm) canvas for apron

9 x 29 in. (23 x 74 cm) canvas for pocket

3¼ yds. (3 m) of 1-in. (2.5-cm) cotton herringbone webbing tape for binding

2 yds. (1.75 m) of 1-in. (2.5-cm) cotton herringbone webbing tape for straps

paper for pattern

pencil

sewing machine and thread

pins

1 Using the shape in the drawing as a guide, cut out a paper pattern, bearing in mind that the length of the apron is 36 in. (92 cm), the width at the bottom is 29 in. (74 cm) and the width of the bib at the top is 11 in. (28 cm).

2 Lay the pattern on the fabric and cut it out. Hem the top edge of the pocket, position it on the front of the apron, turn under the unbound edges, and pin and stitch it in place.

3 Sew cotton webbing tape around the apron to prevent it from fraying. Stitch down the pocket at regular intervals to divide it into sections. Cut two 35-in. (89-cm) lengths of cotton webbing tape for the straps. Pin in place at the top corners of the apron, crossing over at the back.

4 Stitch the straps to the apron, making sure you do not twist the tape as you do so and allowing enough slack for the straps to fit loosely over the body.

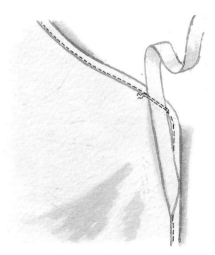

linen-covered journal

A journal is handy to keep notes and lists and stick in
photographs, mementos, and scraps of fabric or wool. This
linen cover not only looks stylish and elegant, but is also
removable for easy washing. By the time journals are full they
tend to double in size, so the ribbon ties attached to the cover
will keep your precious collection together.

MATERIALS

hard-cover journal or notebook
pre-shrunk linen
needle and thread
length of ¾-in. (2-cm) ribbon for tie

1 Lay the journal on the fabric, allowing ½ in. (1 cm) all around for hems and about 3 in. (7.5 cm) at each side for the pockets.

2 Open the journal flat, center it on the fabric, and mark where the book starts and finishes. Cut a ½-in. (1-cm) vertical slit at each point, fold up the fabric twice, and hem. Make a double hem along each short side of the cover.

3 Hem neatly all around the fabric, mitering the corners (see page 16). Place the fabric right side up, with the journal on top of it, fold over the flaps and pin them in position. Remove the journal and sew the top and bottom of the flaps securely.

4 Turn the cover right side out and fit it on the journal. Cut a length of ribbon long enough to go all around the journal plus about 12 in. (30 cm) extra. Fold it in half lengthwise to mark the center and stitch it securely to the center of the spine.

frayed napkins

Frayed edges are back in fashion. These napkins, made from a pretty evenweave fabric printed with a lavender-color design, could not be simpler to create. The same method could be used to make a matching tablecloth.

MATERIALS

18-in. (45-cm) square of evenweave fabric such as linen

sewing machine

needle and matching thread

1 Cut the fabric to the required size—our napkins are *18 in. (45 cm)* square.

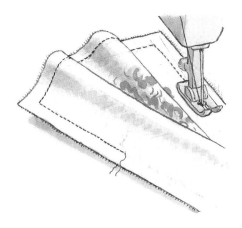

2 Machine stitch around all sides of the fabric about ½ in. (1 cm) from the edge to prevent it fraying further.

3 Using the tip of a needle, carefully pull the threads around the edges to make even amounts of fraying.

picnic basket

These lined baskets make perfect presents—either given empty as picnic baskets or filled with amusing gifts. Ideal for country or beach picnic jaunts, the sturdy cotton liner is washable and can cope with any accidents or spills as you dine al fresco. You could also evoke the wholesome comfort of days gone by and create a vintage-style "Householder's Basket," with wooden clothespins and lavender-scented laundry water. For all the efficiency of today's home gadgets, yesterday's tools of work in the home had a certain comely beauty which still appeals today.

MATERIALS

wire or wicker basket

tape measure

paper for making patterns

cotton fabric

pins

needle and matching thread

1-in. (2.5-cm) cotton webbing tape for ties

1 Measure the depth and circumference of your basket and make a paper pattern, adding 1 in. (2.5 cm) all around for seams and hems. Make a paper pattern for the base of the basket in the same way. Lay your paper pattern on the fabric and cut it out. (You may need to join several pieces to get a piece big enough to fit around the circumference; if so, remember to allow extra for the seams.)

2 Join the fabric pieces for the sides of the basket into a ring. Pin the base piece to the ring, right sides together, and stitch, taking a ¼-in (6-mm) seam.

3 Turn over a ¼-in. (6-mm) double hem on the top of the lining and stitch. If you are using a wire basket, you need to repeat Steps 1 and 2 to make a second liner, then place one inside the other, wrong sides together, so that the reverse of the fabric is not visible through the wire.

4 Cut eight 4-in (10-cm) strips of 1-in. (2.5-cm) cotton tape for the ties. If you are using a double lining, pin pairs of ties at equal intervals between the two linings and stitch around the top edge of the linings to secure. For a single lining, stitch the pairs of ties neatly to the wrong side of the lining.

child's play tent

Of all the ideas in this book this tent is the simplest and possibly the most enchanting. It does not provide any protection from the elements, but it is the perfect present for an adventurous child who wants to play at (supervised) "camping" in the garden. Use sturdy canvas, printed with a full-blown rose pattern both inside and out, and stitch a pocket of contrasting fabric in each corner to hold a heavy weight to prevent the tent from moving in the wind.

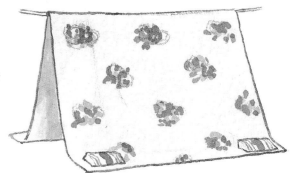

MATERIALS

approx. 2 x 4 yds (2 x 4 m) of heavy canvas fabric

four 12 x 9 in. (30 x 23 cm) pieces of contrasting heavy canvas for pockets

sewing machine

matching thread

strong string or washing line

4 bricks or other heavy objects

1 Make a single miter at each corner of the tent fabric (see page 16) and hem all around.

2 Miter the corners of the four pieces of fabric for the pockets and hem all around.

3 Stitch one pocket to each corner of the outside of the tent, so that a brick or heavy object sits on its long side on the ground.

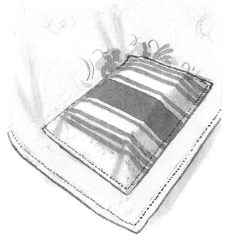

4 Tie the string
or washing line around two
trees or strong supports at a height
of about 4½ ft (1.4 m). Throw the
canvas fabric over the string. Place
a brick or other heavy object in
each pocket to weight the sides
down to the ground. Always super-
vise children when they are at play.

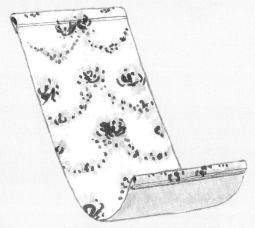

deck-chair slings

Here is a simple way to rejuvenate your old deck chairs with fresh clean slings, giving them a new lease on life. Make sure your deck-chair frame can be taken apart and put together again safely: Usually you can unscrew the top and bottom support of the deck chair in order to slip the old cover off and the new one on, but if this is not possible, cut off the old sling and staple on the new one using a heavy-duty staple gun.

MATERIALS

strong, pre-shrunk canvas
needle and strong thread
sewing machine

1 Measure the width and length of your existing deck-chair sling and add about 4 in (10 cm) to the top and bottom.

2 Cut out the canvas, turn under ½ in. (1 cm) on all four sides, and hem.

3 Measure the wooden bars around which the sling is wrapped and fold over enough fabric at the top and bottom of the fabric to enclose them completely. (Remember to leave enough slack to feed the wooden bar into the slot.) Sew a double line of stitches to hold the slot in place (remember that the sling will have to bear the weight of a fully grown adult).

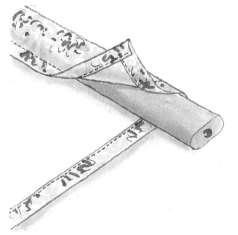

4 Slip the new sling onto the deck-chair frame and reassemble the chair.

beach rug

This reversible rug is an essential for family days
out to the ocean shore. Not only can you lie on the
toweling side and dry yourself, but you can then flip the rug over
and use the waterproof side as a picnic cloth. The toweling can be
removed and washed, while the oilcloth side can simply be wiped
clean. There is also a toweling pocket in which to store car keys,
seashell treasures, or damp swimsuits.

MATERIALS

toweling or ready-made beach towel:
53 x 53 in. (135 x 135 cm) plus an
8-in (20-cm) square for pocket

53 x 53 in. (135 x 135 cm) oilcloth

40 in (100 cm) of 1-in (2.5-cm) Velcro

sewing machine

needle and thread

strong waterproof glue (optional)

pins

1 Lay out the oilcloth, wrong side up, turn over a small hem all around, and either machine stitch or glue in place with a strong waterproof glue.

2 Cut an 8-in. (20-cm) square piece of toweling, hem one edge, and turn under the other three edges. Pin the pocket to one corner of the large piece of toweling or ready-made beach towel and stitch it in place.

3 Lay the large piece of toweling or beach towel right side up on top of the oilcloth. Turn under the hems if the toweling is not already hemmed.

4 Cut the Velcro into 2-in. (5-cm) lengths. Stitch the smooth half of the Velcro strips to the wrong side of the toweling and the gripper side to the wrong side of the oilcloth, spacing them evenly around the edge.

notes

index

acknowledgments

The author would like to thank:

Brigette Buchanan, Tony & Sabrina Fry, Ali Sharland, Helen Blackman, Liz Thompson, Lena Proudlock, Kate Strutt, Max Linham, Georgina Harris, Cindy Richards, Sarah Hoggett, Kate Simunek, Edina van der Wyck, Matthew Tugwell and my infinitely patient family—all of whom have played huge practical and inspirational roles in the production of this book.

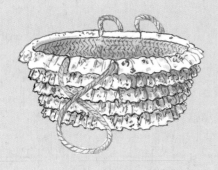